ANIMALS
That Make a Difference!

Bats
박쥐

Ashley Lee

Explore other books at:
WWW.ENGAGEBOOKS.COM

VANCOUVER, B.C.

e → WWW.ENGAGEBOOKS.COM

Bats: Level 1 Bilingual (English/Korean) (영어/한국어)
Animals That Make a Difference!
Lee, Ashley 1995 —
Text © 2021 Engage Books
Edited by: A.R. Roumanis
and Lauren Dick
Translated by: Gio Oh
Proofread by: Tamara Kazali

Text set in Arial Regular.
Chapter headings set in Arial Black.

FIRST EDITION / FIRST PRINTING

LIBRARY AND ARCHIVES CANADA CATALOGUING IN PUBLICATION

Title: Animals That Make a Difference: Bats Level 1 Bilingual (English/Korean) (영어/한국어)
Names: Lee, Ashley, author.

ISBN 978-1-77476-449-7 (hardcover)
ISBN 978-1-77476-448-0 (softcover)

Subjects:
LCSH: Bats—Juvenile literature
LCSH: Human-animal relationships—Juvenile literature

Classification: LCC QL737.C5 L44 2020 | DDC J599.4—DC23

Contents
목차

3

What Are Bats?
박쥐는 무엇인가요?

Bats are the only mammals that can fly.
박쥐는 날 수 있는 유일한 포유류에요.

Mammals are covered in hair
and have bones in their back.
They feed their babies milk.
포유류는 털로 덮여 있고 등에 뼈가
있어요. 그들은 새끼들에게 젖을
먹여요.

What Do Bats Look Like?
박쥐는 어떻게 생겼나요?

The smallest bats are only 6 inches (15 centimeters) wide. The largest bats can be up to 6 feet (1.8 meters) wide.

가장 작은 박쥐는 폭이 6인치(15센티미터) 넓이에 불과해요. 가장 큰 박쥐는 폭이 6피트(1.8미터) 나 됩니다.

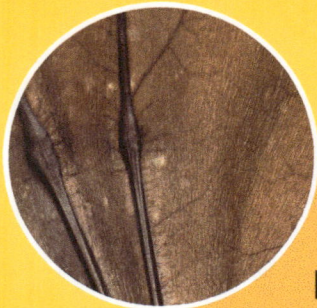

Bat wings are made of thin skin. The skin is stretched between the front and back legs.

박쥐의 날개는 얇은 가죽으로 되어있어요. 가죽은 앞다리와 뒷다리까지 이어져있어요.

A bat's ears are large compared to the size of its head. Bats use their ears to find food and other bats.
박쥐의 귀는 머리크기에 비해서 큰편이에요. 박쥐는 먹이를 찾거나 다른 박쥐를 찾기위해 귀를 사용해요.

Bats have claws on their feet. They use their claws to hold things.
박쥐는 발에 발톱이 있어요. 발톱은 물건을 잡기 위해 사용해요.

Where Do Bats Live?
박쥐는 어디에 사나요?

Bats make homes called roosts. Roosts are used for sleeping. Most bats make roosts in caves or old buildings.

박쥐의 집은 둥지라고 불러요. 둥지는 잠을 자는데 사용돼요. 대부분 박쥐는 동굴이나 오래된 건물에 둥지를 짓습니다.

Most bats live in tropical areas. Tube-nosed bats live in Australia. Indian flying fox bats live in India. Sulawesi fruit bats come from Indonesia.

대부분 박쥐는 열대 지방에 살아요. 관코박쥐는 호주에 살아요. 인도 여우날박쥐는 인도에 살아요. 과일 박쥐는 인도네시아에 살아요.

Indonesia
인도네시아

Europe
유럽

Asia
아시아

India
인도

Pacific
Ocean
태평양

Africa
아프리카

Atlantic
Ocean
대서양

Australia
호주

Australia
호주

Southern
Ocean
남대양

2,000 miles
2,000 마일
0

4,000 kilometers
4,000 킬로미터
0

N

Legend 전설
Land 육지
Ocean 바다

9

What Do Bats Eat?
박쥐는 무엇을 먹나요?

Most bats eat fruit or insects. Some bats drink a sweet liquid from flowers called nectar. A few bats eat small animals. They eat birds, frogs, and lizards.

대부분 박쥐들은 과일이나 곤충을 먹어요. 어떤 박쥐들은 꿀, 넥타라고 불리는 꽃에서 나온 달콤한 액체를 마셔요. 소수의 박쥐들은 작은 동물을 먹기도해요. 쥐, 개구리 그리고 도마뱀을 먹어요.

Some bats find food by using special cries. These cries bounce back to the bat when they hit an object. Bats hear their cry and can tell where small animals are. This is called echolocation.

어떤 박쥐들은 특별한 울음으로 음식을 찾기도 해요. 이 울음은 물체를 치고 박쥐에게 돌아와요. 박쥐는 이 울음을듣고 작은 동물이 어디 있는지 알 수 있어요. 이것은 반향위치측정이라고 불려요.

How Do Bats Talk to Each Other?
박쥐는 서로 어떻게 이야기 하나요?

Bats use chirps and cries to talk to each other. They use these sounds to find other bats or warn others of danger.
박쥐는 서로 소통하기 위해서 울음을 사용해요. 박쥐는 이 소리로 다른 박쥐를 찾거나 위험을 경고해주기 위해서 사용해요.

Some bat sounds are so high-pitched they cannot be heard by people.
어떤 울음은 인간이 들을 수 없는 아주 높은 소리에요.

Bat Life Cycle
박쥐의 일생

Baby bats are called pups. They learn to fly when they are 3 weeks old.
아기 박쥐 즉, 새끼 박쥐는 태어난지 3 주가 됐을 때 나는 것을 배워요.

Pups stay in groups called nurseries. They are cared for by female bats.
새끼 박쥐는 암컷 박쥐가 돌봐주는 유치원 같은 곳에서 지내요.

Pups are fully grown at 2 months old. This is when they leave the nursery.
태어난지 2달이 되면 새끼 박쥐는 성체가 돼요. 그때 유치원을 떠나요.

Most bats live for 10 to 20 years. Very few bats live more than 30 years.
대부분 박쥐는 10년에서 20년을 살아요. 소수의 박쥐들은 30년을 살기도 해요.

Curious Facts About Bats

Bats lick themselves
to keep clean.
박쥐는 몸을 핥아서
청결을 유지해요.

The oldest known living
bat was 41 years old.
가장 오래 산 박쥐는
41살이에요.

Bats can eat more than
1,000 insects in an hour.
박쥐는 한시간 동안 1,000
마리 이상의 곤충을 먹을
수 있어요.

박쥐에 대한 흥미로운 사실들

Some bats sleep through winter. This is called hibernation.
박쥐는 겨울 동안 잠을 자요. 이걸 겨울잠이라고 해요.

Most bats sleep upside down. They hang from their feet.
대부분 박쥐는 거꾸로 잠을 자요. 발로 매달려 있어요.

Bat knees bend backwards.
박쥐의 무릎은 거꾸로 접혀요.

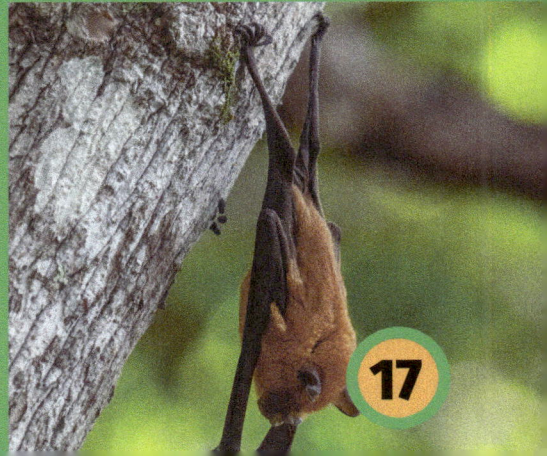

17

Kinds of Bats
박쥐의 종류

There are more than 1,300 kinds of bats. These are split into two groups. Microbats eat insects. They usually only come out at night.

박쥐 종류는 1,300종이 넘어요. 이들은 두 갈래로 나눌 수 있어요. 작은 박쥐류는 곤충을 먹어요. 그리고 밤에만 활동한답니다.

Megabats eat fruit and nectar. They have larger eyes than microbats. Some megabats come out during the day.
큰박쥐류는 과일이나 꽃에 있는 꿀을 먹어요. 작은 박쥐류보다 큰 눈을 가지고 있어요. 몇몇은 낮에도 나와서 활동해요.

How Bats Help Earth
박쥐가 지구를 돕는 방법

Bats eat many plant seeds. The seeds come out in their poop. Bat poop helps seeds grow into new plants.
박쥐는 씨앗을 많이 먹어요. 그 씨앗이 박쥐의 똥을 통해서 나와요. 박쥐의 똥은 식물이 새로 자랄 수 있게 도와요.

Pollen is a fine powder that flowers make. Female plants need pollen from male plants to make seeds. Bats help spread pollen from one plant to another. This is called pollination.

꽃가루는 꽃이 만드는 고운 가루에요. 암그루는 씨앗을 만들기 위해 수그루에게서 나온 꽃가루가 필요해요. 박쥐는 이 식물에서 저 식물에게 꽃가루를 옮겨줘요. 이를 수분이라고 해요.

How Bats Help
Other Animals
박쥐가 다른 동물을 돕는 방법

Many animals eat the plants that bats help grow. These animals would have less food to eat without bats.

많은 동물들은 박쥐가 자라는 것을 도와준 식물을 먹어요. 박쥐의 도움이 없었다면 동물들의 먹이가 적었을 거에요.

Desert animals drink water from cacti. Some cacti can only grow if bats pollinate them. Desert animals would not have enough water without bats.

사막에 사는 동물은 선인장에서 나오는 물을 마셔요. 어떤 선인장은 박쥐가 수분을 해줘야만 자랄 수 있어요. 박쥐가 없었다면 사막의 동물은 물이 부족했을 거에요.

23

How Bats Help Humans
박쥐가 사람을 돕는 방법

Bats eat insects that harm the food humans grow. They also pollinate fruits and vegetables. There would be fewer bananas, avocados, and mangoes without bats.

박쥐는 사람이 기르는 음식을 해치는 벌레를 잡아먹어요. 박쥐는 채소나 과일도 수분을 해줍니다. 박쥐 없이는 바나나, 아보카도, 망고가 훨씬 적었을 거에요.

Scientists are making a new medicine from bat drool. The medicine is called Draculin. It is helping people with heart problems.

과학자들은 박쥐의 침을 사용해서 새로운 약을 만들고있어요. 이 약은 드라큘린이라고 불립니다. 이 약은 심장 질환을 가지고 있는 사람들을 돕는 약이에요.

Bats in Danger
멸종위기의 박쥐

Many bats are endangered. This means there are very few of them left. A disease called white-nose syndrome is making bats end their hibernation early. When bats wake up, there is not enough food to eat.

많은 박쥐들이 멸종위기에요. 박쥐가 많이 남지 않았다는 말이에요. 박쥐가 수분을 빨리 끝내게 하는 병은 흰색 코 증후군이라 불러요. 박쥐가 잠에서 깨면 충분한 먹이가 없어요.

Some bats are hunted by humans.
The Mauritian flying fox bat is hunted on
Mauritius island. The country sees the bats
as pests. These bats are disappearing.
몇몇 박쥐들은 인간에 의해 사냥당해요.
모리셔스 날 여우 박쥐는 모리셔스 섬에서
사냥당해요. 그 섬에서는 박쥐를 해충으로
여겨요. 이 박쥐들은 사라지고 있어요.

How To Help Bats
박쥐를 돕는 방법

Pesticides are chemicals that kill bugs.
Bats eat insects that have been sprayed
with pesticides. This can make bats very sick.
Many people are no longer using pesticides.

농약은 벌레를 죽이는 화학약품이에요. 농약에
맞은 벌레를 박쥐가 먹어요. 이는 박쥐를 매우
아프게 만들어요. 많은 사람들이 더 이상 농약을
사용하지 않아요.

Some people do not like bats. They will scare bats away from their homes. Tell your friends and family how helpful bats are. This can help save bats from being forced out of their roosts.

어떤 사람들은 박쥐를 싫어해요. 그래서 박쥐를 집에서 쫓아내기도 해요. 가족과 친구들에게 박쥐가 얼마나 유용한지 전해주세요. 보금자리에서 쫓겨나는 박쥐들을 구할 수도 있어요.

Quiz
퀴즈

Test your knowledge of bats by answering the following questions. The questions are based on what you have read in this book. The answers are listed on the bottom of the next page.
밑의 질문들에 대답을 하면서 박쥐에 대한 지식을 테스트 해보세요. 질문은 위에서 읽은 내용에 기초합니다. 정답은 다음 페이지에 적혀있어요.

1 What are bat wings made of?
박쥐의 날개는 무엇으로 만들어졌나요?

2 What are bat homes called?
박쥐의 집은 뭐라고 불리나요?

3 What are baby bats called?
아기 박쥐는 뭐라고 불리나요?

4 How do most bats sleep?
대부분 박쥐는 어떻게 자나요?

5 How many kinds of bats are there?
얼마나 많은 박쥐의 종류가 있나요?

6 What are pesticides?
농약은 무엇인가요?

Explore other books in the Animals That Make a Difference series.

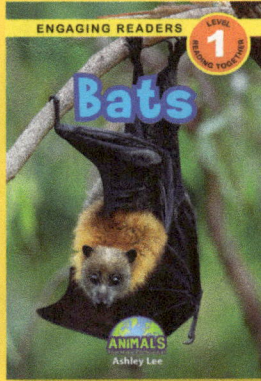

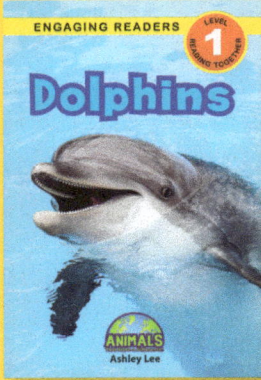

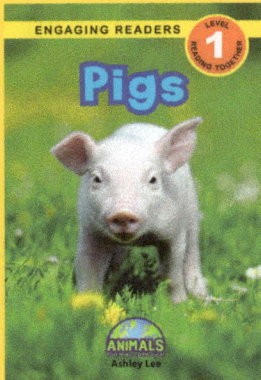

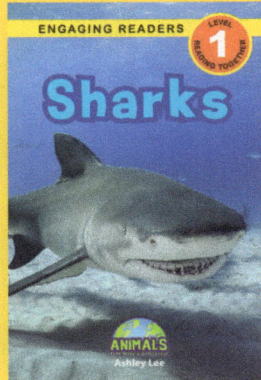

ENGAGING READERS — LEVEL 1 — Bees — *Jared Siemens*

ENGAGING READERS — LEVEL 1 — Bats — *Ashley Lee*

ENGAGING READERS — LEVEL 1 — Birds — *Ashley Lee*

ENGAGING READERS — LEVEL 1 — Dolphins — *Ashley Lee*

ENGAGING READERS — LEVEL 1 — Horses — *Ashley Lee*

ENGAGING READERS — LEVEL 1 — Ladybugs — *Ashley Lee*

ENGAGING READERS — LEVEL 1 — Pigs — *Ashley Lee*

ENGAGING READERS — LEVEL 1 — Sharks — *Ashley Lee*

ENGAGING READERS — LEVEL 1 — Squirrels — *Ashley Lee*

Visit www.engagebooks.com to explore more Engaging Readers.

Answers:
1. Thin skin 2. Roosts 3. Pups 4. Upside down 5. More than 1,300 6. Chemicals that kill bugs

정답:
1. 얇은 가죽 2. 둥지 3. 새끼박쥐 4. 거꾸로 5. 1,300종 이상 6. 벌레를 죽이는 화학 약품

www.ingramcontent.com/pod-product-compliance
Lightning Source LLC
Chambersburg PA
CBHW051234020426
42331CB00016B/3374